Kant & Natural Law

Ethics Study Guide

Peter Baron

First published 2012

by PushMe Press

Mid Somerset House, Southover, Wells, Somerset BA5 1UH

www.pushmepress.com

British Library Cataloguing in Publication Data
A catalogue record for this book is available from the British Library

ISBN: 978-1-909618-02-2 (pbk)
ISBN: 978-1-909618-09-3(ebk)
ISBN: 978-1-78484-010-5 (hbk)
ISBN: 978-1-910252-37-6(pdf)

Typeset in Frutiger by booksellerate.com
Printed by Lightning Source

A rich and engaging community assisted by the best teachers in Ethics

ethics.pushmepress.com

Students and teachers explore Ethics through handouts, film clips, presentations, case studies, extracts, games and academic articles.

Pitched just right, and so much more than a textbook, here is a place to engage with critical reflection whatever your level. Marked student essays are also posted.

Contents

Introduction

DEONTOLOGICAL ethics is the ethics of duty and rules (deon = duty in Greek). The three theories usually described as deontological in A level syllabuses are Kantian ethics, Natural Law and Divine Command Theory, although only the first and third of these are pure deontology. Natural Law, I will argue, should be considered as a theory with both **DEONTOLOGICAL** and **TELEOLOGICAL** aspects.

ANALYSING THEORIES

To analyse ethical theories we will ask four questions which spell the acronym **DARM**.

- **DERIVATION** - How is the idea of goodness derived? Where does it come from? What is the logic and line of reasoning? What assumptions are being made? What worldview forms the idea of good?

- **APPLICATION** - Having decided where good comes from, how do we apply the idea to real world events and choices? What principles are involved? How do we think the theory through to produce a practical decision?

- **REALISM** - A theory can appear fine on paper, but how does it fit with our understanding of human nature? Does it makes sense to me, as someone who is supposed to reason about moral choices? Does it seem to correspond with what other disciplines such as psychology are suggesting? If not it may be better to discard the theory.

- **MOTIVATION** - A basic question we need to answer is: why should I be moral? Why should I care about my neighbour, or the starving in Africa? Why not just be an egoist, living for self and using others for my own ends?

HOW DEONTOLOGY WORKS

Deontological theories attempt to give us rules for living. One issue is how hard and fast these rules can be. In this book, we examine two theories, rather different in their approach, the absolute deontology of Kant and the teleological deontology of Natural Law, but we also consider WD Ross' theory of prima facie duties (duties grasped at first sight - prima facie - which are not absolute duties, but depend for their application on the situation).

Kantian ethics attempts to derive **A PRIORI PRINCIPLES** using the process of reason alone. Kant believed every human mind was set up the same way, and so would reach the same conclusions if we applied our reason to the same relevant circumstances. He believed we could establish rules that were absolute and allowed no exceptions, and are universal, applying to everyone.

Kant's is an argument about intrinsic goodness or what is good in itself. He argues that to act in the morally right way we must act from duty alone, not from feeling or intuition. Kant opposed David Hume who argued that "feelings are the slave of the passions". The highest good, argues Kant, must be both good in itself and good without qualification. To be "good without qualification" means that when we act on this motive, we never makes a situation ethically worse.

Kant sees those things that are usually thought to be good such as happiness or pleasure, fail to be either intrinsically good (because our actions are a means to an end - pleasure) or good without qualification (because when we maximise pleasure we often do others harm - those whose pain is less than the pleasure we are maximising). For example, when people take pleasure in causing someone pain, such as playing music excessively loud at a party at night, this makes the situation ethically worse. Kant concludes that there is only one thing that is truly good, and that is our motive:

> *"Nothing in the world - indeed nothing even beyond the world - can possibly be conceived which could be called good without qualification except a good will."*

Natural law theory starts in a very different place with human beings and their rational natures. How are these natures ordered? What ends do we pursue? What are our aims in life?

Natural law theory predicts that all rational beings will pursue the same general ends. So we can observe what these ends are. Although this sounds teleological, and arises out of the Greek teleological worldview, Thomas Aquinas argues that the outcome is to produce laws (rules) which correspond to the divine law.

Just as Kantian ethics has an outcome in mind, the summum bonum or greatest good, so Natural Law has an ultimate end - human flourishing or **EUDAIMONIA** in Greek. The difference between them is important though. Kant emphasises the intrinsic goodness of the motive or "good will", whereas Aquinas emphasises the **TELEOLOGICAL** end of human flourishing achieved by exercising practical wisdom.

AN INTERACTIVE APPROACH

From deontological ethics we gain some valuable insights about how to live. These insights we will call here the ethics toolkit. In practice, though deontological and teleological theories sound rather different, there is considerable overlap between them. For example, the rich concept of eudaimonia (usually translated "flourishing"), central to Natural Law, is also considered as central to many pure teleological theories - Mill's utilitarianism being one. Interestingly, Mill accused Kant of being a utilitarian in deontologist's clothing because with Kant's key idea, universalisability, Mill felt it was impossible to universalise without considering the likely consequences.

The insights of Kantian rationality and Natural Law purposefulness, both **DEONTOLOGICAL** forms of morality, can equip us with two important methods of ethics to allow us to think more deeply about moral issues and the dilemmas we face today. In this interactive approach, we consider how scenes from films illustrate the nature of deontological ethics and suggest self-assessment exercises to strengthen your understanding.

Kantian Ethics

"Kantian Ethics is one of the most beautiful creations that the human mind has ever devised." Roger Scruton

"Pure practical reason requires not that we should renounce the claims of happiness; it requires only that we take no account of them when whenever duty is in question." Immanuel Kant

Kant (1724-1802) is often described as the father of liberalism and the key philosopher of the Enlightenment. He never married and never travelled further than 20 miles from his native town of Koningsberg in north Prussia (modern Kaliningrad in Russia). Nonetheless his philosophy and ethics produced a revolution in favour of the dignity, equality and rights of every person.

Roger Scruton calls Kantian Ethics "one of the most beautiful creations that the human mind has ever devised", (1996:284) because Kantian ethics has an elegant logic and consistency. Kant believed that when I say "killing is wrong", I imply "everyone ought not to kill", a universal absolute. This applies to all rational beings, everywhere, for all time.

However Kant also believed that a moral principle could be generated a priori, which means "before experience". This means the idea of "goodness" is independent of someone's needs or desires, which can only be known a posteriori, "after experience".

Kant's great project was to prove that reason alone can generate a moral principle such as "thou shalt not kill", whose validity is not subjective, but objective (valid for all people everywhere and at any time).

This morality, he argues, is built on practical reason alone, and nothing else: a type of reasoning which is very different from scientific reasoning, for example, which he calls "pure reason", because practical reason belongs purely to the realm of ideas.

The Kantian Worldview

ENLIGHTENMENT

The Enlightenment began with the Protestant revolution of the 1530s, a protest against autocratic rule by Popes and Monarchs, with a focus on the individual and the power of educated reason. Kant adopted the Enlightenment motto "Dare to Reason". Just as the the Enlightenment rejected the old structures of authority and the hierarchy with God at the top and instead placed the individual and reason at the centre, so Kant rejected outside influences on human reason (called **HETERONOMY**) in favour of an **AUTONOMY** (self-rule) which honours humanity.

> *"I am an inquirer by inclination. I feel a consuming thirst for knowledge, the unrest which goes with the desire to progress in it, and satisfaction at every advance in it. There was a time when I believed this constituted the honour of humanity, and I despised the people, who know nothing. Rousseau set me right about this. This binding prejudice disappeared. I learned to honour humanity, and I would find myself more useless than the common labourer if I did not believe that this attitude of mine can give worth to all others in establishing the rights of humanity." Immanuel Kant*

THE LOGIC OF KANT

Kant's argument has a faultless logic that starts with the idea of human autonomy (freedom or self-rule). There are a number of steps he takes to establish the idea of what is good and bad.

1. We are free (autonomous or self-ruled).

2. This freedom means we can choose to act from reason alone, overruling desires and emotions.

3. The form of reason used is a priori reasoning, that doesn't depend on desires or feelings, but only on abstract reasoning, like mathematics. This is then applied to the real world of experience (the truth is synthetic, meaning true by experience, not analytic, meaning true by definition).

4. The only thing good in itself is the good will, because any other motive for acting, such as happiness or pleasure is corrupted by desire and emotion, which are fickle things, subject to change and circumstance, so only good in a qualified way.

5. So the only moral act is one from duty alone, using reason to work out what is right and wrong.

6. The a priori principle all rational people will come up with is called the Categorical Imperative which means "an unconditional command".

7. This imperative has three forms, the principle of law, the principle of ends, and the principle of autonomy. In applying these we arrive at maxims or subjective rules for action.

8. The principle of law says we should universalise our actions and turn them into a universal law, so that what I believe is wrong is also wrong for everyone else.

9. The principle of ends universalises our humanity and says: treat everyone as if they had the same dignity and freedom as you do.

10. The principle of autonomy asks us to imagine we are the sole ruler. What laws would we come up with that could be applied to everyone, irrespective of gender, colour, financial situation etc?

11. So we have our absolute principle (the categorical imperative) which we can apply to the real (synthetic) world to generate rules of conduct and ideas of moral goodness.

KANTIAN WORLDVIEW

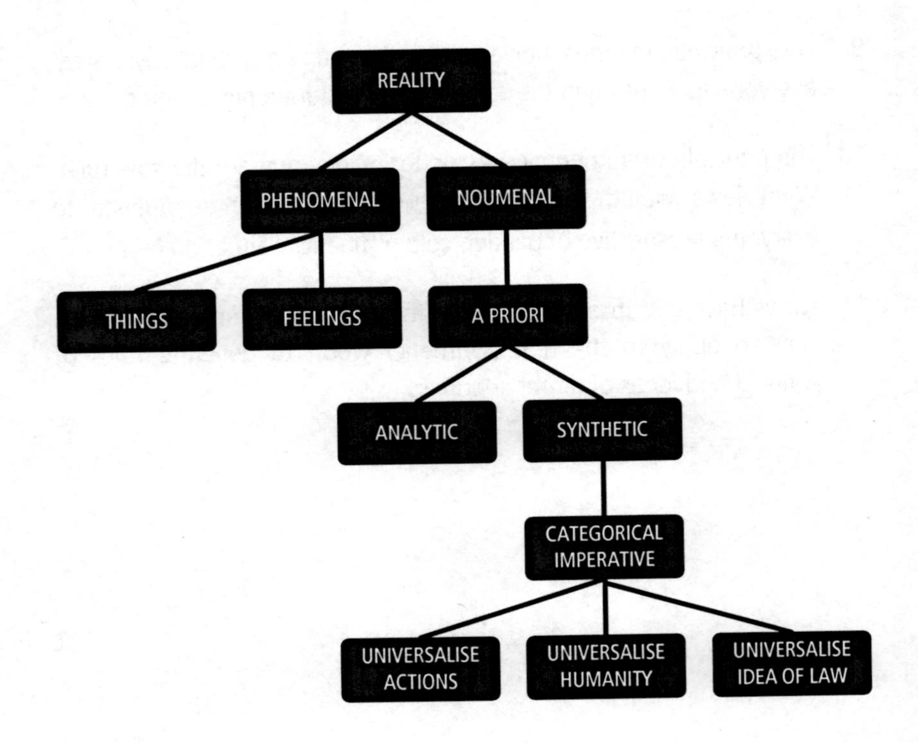

THE THREE POSTULATES

Kant said there were three postulates or necessary conditions for morality. These are things Kant assumes but never proves.

1. **FREEDOM**

   Human beings are rational, free, self-legislators. We create the moral law for ourselves by a process of reasoning.

"Freedom, however, is the only one of all the ideas of the speculative reason of which we know the possibility a priori (without, however, understanding it), because it is the condition of the moral law which we know."

2. **IMMORTALITY**

   Immortality is a necessary postulate because we are commanded to be perfect and attain the summum bonum. Since "ought" implies "can" we must be able to reach moral perfection. But we cannot attain perfection in this life, for the task is an infinite one, so there must be an afterlife, in which to continue to make progress to this ideal.

"The achievement of the highest good in the world is the necessary object of a will determinable by the moral law. In such a will however the complete fitness of intentions to the moral law is the supreme condition of the highest good. The fitness, therefore, must be just as possible as its object ... But complete fitness of the will to the moral law is holiness, which is a perfection of which no rational being in the world of sense is at

any time capable. But since it is required as practical necessity it can only be found in endless progress to that complete fitness. This infinite progress is possible however, only on the presupposition of an infinitely enduring existence and personality of the same rational being; this is called the immortality of the soul. Thus the highest good is practically possible only on the supposition of the immortality of the soul ... God."

3. **GOD**

God is also a necessary postulate because there must be someone to enforce the moral law. Someone is needed to judge to reward the virtuous and to punish the evil.

"The same law must also lead us to affirm the possibility of the second element of the highest good, ie happiness proportional to that morality. This we can do on the supposition of the existence of a cause adequate to this effect. It must postulate the existence of God as necessarily belonging to the possibility of the highest good."

SUMMUM BONUM

Kant rejected happiness as a primary goal in moral decision making. He rejected both the Stoic view of the world, that only duty mattered, and the Epicurean view, that happiness was the supreme goal. He argued instead for a deontological ethics of duty, but with one outcome in mind - that by being moral each of us make our own small contribution to building a better world.

> *"Pure practical reason requires not that we should renounce the claims of happiness; it requires only that we take no account of them when whenever duty is in question."*

However happiness is something that we necessarily pursue as rational beings. For Kant happiness amounts to the satisfaction of our inclinations. The **SUMMUM BONUM** or highest good consists of two parts, virtue and happiness. Virtue - connected to the "Good Will" is the required condition for anything to be good or desirable. For Kant virtue means dutifulness or unconditional commitment to the moral law. But this does not mean that virtue is the "entire and perfect good", rather, "for this happiness is also required".

The perfect state for Kant would be one in which humans are happy to the degree that they deserve to be happy - duty (virtue) has its own reward.

REASON OR FEELING

David Hume argued that feeling was the source of all moral judgment. "Reason is the slave of the passions," he wrote. It was the feeling of sympathy which guided our moral choices, an idea which JS Mill also argued for in his essay on Utilitarianism. Kant rejected this argument, seeing feelings as fickle and unreliable.

> *"The highest created good is the most perfect world, that is a world in which rational beings are happy and are worthy of happiness." Immanuel Kant*

Inspirations for Kant

TWO INSPIRATIONS - NEWTON AND ROUSSEAU

Kant was inspired by Isaac Newton to look for a rational revolution in ethics, and by Rousseau to put equality, dignity and absolute respect for human beings at the heart of his theory.

The 18th C was a period of philosophy when Natural Law was dominant. Natural Law held that morality derived from the nature of the world and of human beings. Human beings had a function, to exercise reason, but they exercised this reason very much in line with the principles of science: they made deductions from observation and proceeded a posteriori (from experience).

How might this work?

I observe that human beings are social animals who also seem to abide by certain rules in ordering the conduct of the group. It seems important to them to maximise the happiness and welfare of the group, and protect itself from harm, danger and pain, or anything that upsets group harmony and coexistence.

From this we can observe certain naturalistic features of morality, features of the natural world. For example, we observe features of human beings and their minds, such as the presence of guilt and shame which deters some behaviour, and the response to praise which reinforces others.

So we can produce a list of things which are good, generated by the role of human beings exercising their choices in order to realise the value of the happiness and welfare of the group (and so in sense defining these things as "good" or "desirable").

Natural Law theorists might differ as to what is on the list. For example, Aristotle's list might be different from Aquinas' list, partly because Aquinas was a Christian who believed that the reasonable person would always end up agreeing with the view of God found in the Bible, who is the source of reason and sets the standard for reasonableness.

But it is the method which is important here: proceeding from observation to inferences about what constitutes the good: an a posteriori way of reasoning dependent on the real world of our senses.

KANT'S ANSWER TO NATURAL LAW

Kant wrote:

> *"... two things fill the mind with ever new and increasing admiration ... the starry heavens above me and the moral law within."*

Here he is paying tribute to two approaches to reasoning, the pure scientific reason and the **A PRIORI** practical reason.

The starry heavens are a tribute to Newton and the advances in scientific discovery using the scientific method of observing things and then working out laws from this process. If Newton can do this using pure reason operating **A POSTERIORI**, from experience, couldn't Kant fulfil a similar purpose using practical reason operating a priori? Couldn't he provide a groundwork to the metaphysics of morals, where metaphysics means beyond physics, just as Newton had produced a groundwork to the physics of science? As we have noted, the approaches are essentially different, and reason uses a different method with each (or so Kant set out to prove).

The Church with its use of threats of damnation, inquisitions, and influence on law had restricted the free exercise of reason. So although Kant may have believed that some afterlife exists which ultimately rewarded duty, his philosophy was against the oppressive nature of the Church and very much for the free exercise of reason. We are all moral legislators for our own lives, argued Kant, and in so arguing he is the precursor of the great libertarians of the 18th C, such as JS Mill.

Kant's first inspiration was Newton, because Newton showed how reason unleashed could transform our understanding. Kant's second great inspiration was Jean-Jacques Rousseau, who had famously declared "all men are born free, but are everywhere in chains". What Rousseau applied to the political sphere (equality and freedom around a common interest) Kant applied to the moral sphere.

KEY ASSUMPTION - AUTONOMY

Here we encounter Kant's starting point, that we are autonomous moral beings. **AUTONOMOUS** means "self-ruled" and its opposite is **HETERONOMOUS** or "other-ruled". Kant argued that we needed a way of producing moral principles (he called them "maxims") which did not imply we were ruled by another, but were self-ruled (autonomous).

The two **HETERONOMOUS** forces on us, Kant argued, were God and our human emotions (what Hume called "the passions"). Kant believed that our emotions pulled us in different ways, and so opposed Hume's view that "reason is the slave of the passions".

To Kant it was impossible to be rational and follow our passions. Kant often called these passions "pathological" which implies, as Paul said in Romans 7 "the very thing I do not want, this is what I do". There is a kind of war on between the irrational passions and the rational will. To Kant there is a "causality of freedom" implied by the idea of rational choice; as Scruton puts it :

> *"Morality, by presupposing freedom, shows that our freedom is real; all other motives enslave us." (1996:286)*

The Noumenal Realm of Ideas

WHY KANT OPPOSES EMOTION

Kant's imperatives stood against the natural order of emotions. Instead of the argument running like this:

observation → natural human nature → idea of goodness

Kant's argument runs like this:

reason → universal principle → idea of goodness

Kant opposed the rule of feelings as he felt they were likely to change with different circumstances. He argued that morality needed to be consistent and unchanging.

So a Kantian imperative does not say "I ought because I want" but rather "one ought because it's universally right" (the impersonal "one" or "du" in German), and remember "ought implies can" because it is possible in the real world. We do have freedom to choose and power to act.

KANT'S PHILOSOPHY OF MIND

Kant's Critique of Pure Reason explains how our minds order our perceptions and so give knowledge of the outside world. Kant believed all humans shared one common cognitive structure.

Although we think of our experience of seeing as something scientific, it is in fact a metaphysical experience. This is because perception doesn't exist like a television screen: I can't point to a place in the brain where what I'm seeing now is being "transmitted" in a physical sense. What has happened is our brains have ordered our perception, our minds have made sense of the chaotic images hitting the brain.

If I write on my whiteboard the whiteboard is passive: it just receives the pen marks I put on it. But if I type into a computer, it is active (and rather annoyingly this text will jump up a few lines if I accidentally strike the mouse!). These programs are active in the computer.

Kant believed our minds work like the active, programmed computer. The word he used for these is categories. These capacities are inbuilt to human beings (whether by God or by evolution isn't the issue here).

Take the idea of causality. The idea of cause and effect shapes how I interpret things. If I feel a kick in my back, I look round to find the cause. I then interpret what I see (for example, I assume the nearest person kicked me). The idea of causation is an **A PRIORI** law of the mind.

Kant believed in the objective moral law, but not as part of the **PHENOMENAL** world (the world out there) but as one of the categories of the mind. Slightly confusingly, he refers to them as objective laws of our minds which should not be confused with the objective laws of science (which empiricists like Hume believed in).

So to Kant, ethics belongs to the world of the a priori (before experience), the world of categories or "things in themselves". He called this the **NOUMENAL** world. This is a reality behind the reality of our senses - in another sense it makes sense of all the raw sensory data we process by our minds. Our moral laws are like the computer programmes which process what we type in. Ultimately, Kant believed God had designed us like that, but in fact Kantian ethics is quite compatible with modern science which is beginning to realise that reality is not quite as objective as is sometimes implied.

Categories of thought, then, like cause and effect and the moral law, exist as objective laws of the mind, a priori concepts which determine how we make sense of the chaos of reality and experience.

> *"Objective laws relate of necessity and a priori to the objects of experience, because only by means of them can any object of experience be thought". Immanuel Kant*

THE A PRIORI SYNTHETIC

Kant believed ethical statements were a priori synthetic. An analytic statement is true by definition, for example, "all bachelors are unmarried". A synthetic statement is one provable true or false. For example, cause and effect is an a priori idea, but if I feel pain, it may or not be caused by you hitting me (and I can establish whether "you hit me" is true or false). The category is cause and effect, the application is "you hit me" - a synthetic proposition.

PHENOMENAL OR NOUMENAL

Kant believed human experience could be divided between two realms, the realm of ideas and the realm of experience, and that morality came from the realm of ideas.

Kant thought that God, angels and human beings shared in the realm of ideas or the noumenal world which was there to be discovered by our reason. The way we look at morality is structured by the human mind, which is able to understand some things a priori, before any use of our five senses, using practical reason. Much of Mathematics, for example, is understood this way, and when Einstein came up with his theory of relativity this too was an a priori concept. He never did the experiments to prove it was true: he left that to the Cambridge scientists.

The second realm is the realm of the observable and of experience, which Kant calls the phenomenal realm. This part of human experience can be felt, touched, seen, smelt, heard. It includes our emotions, too, which Kant continually contrasts with our reason.

HUMANS SHARE AN ANGELIC AND AN ANIMAL NATURE

Humans access both realms: the noumenal and the phenomenal (see illustration). But morality takes its absolute authority from the noumenal world, and is derived a priori. It is then proved to be true or false by being applied to the world of experience the synthetic. For example, it only makes sense to say "lying is wrong" when confronted with a situation where I am tempted to lie. I must always follow this rule, however, and so, in a sense, conquer my feelings with the supreme good of duty to follow the moral law from the pure motive of the good will. This is what is meant by synthetic a priori.

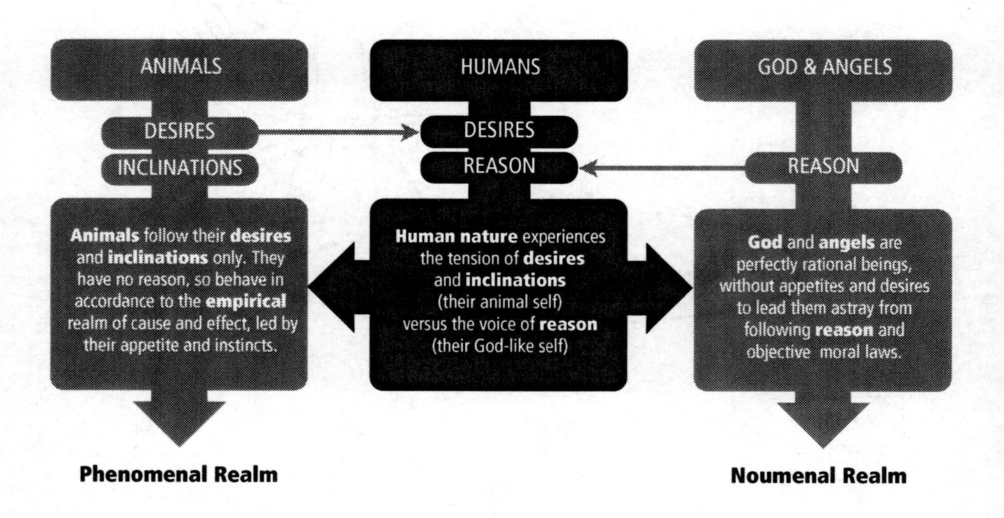

The Good Will and the Categorical Imperative

THE GOOD WILL AND THE GOOD AGENT

Things can have intrinsic good, because they are good in themselves, or instrumental good, because they are a means to something else. Kant argued that the only thing intrinsically good was the good will.

Kant argued that the only thing that is good without qualification is the good will. The good will is never instrumental; it doesn't require a goal or end (such as happiness or love or flourishing). It isn't a means to something else.

> *"The good will shines like a jewel for its own sake as something which has full value in itself."* Kant

Here Kant may be seeming to push his own moral thinking into a corner. Is he really saying an action is only good if done out of a sense of duty to the moral law? Is the only allowable motive the motive of duty? What if I enjoy helping old ladies across the street, or pay my taxes because of self-interest (I don't want to incur the £100 fine for not filling in my tax form)? Does that somehow empty my action of any moral worth?

Can my good will somehow be corrupted by desire or emotion, those two outside influences Kant is trying to set us free from (together of course with freedom from the external "God")?

Here Kant, if we are right in interpreting him this way, is against not just

Hume but also Aristotle and the virtue ethicists. For Aristotle a virtuous person needed to really enjoy the pursuit of friendship, honesty, temperance or courage. If he or she didn't enjoy it, they were not really flourishing, nor were they acting out of their true character.

But are we right to criticise Kant for seeming in places to argue that only an action done out of the motive of duty is morally good? Kenny would argue we are.

> *"We must distinguish between acting in accordance with duty, and acting from the motive of duty. A grocer who is honest from self-interest ... may do actions in accordance with duty. But actions of this kind, however right and amiable, have, according to Kant, no moral worth. Worth of character is shown only when one does good not from inclination, but from duty." (Kenny, 1998:137)*

In a brilliant essay Schneewind (ed. Guyer, 1992:326) argues that the extreme form of duty which allows no exceptions may be a misunderstanding of Kant's position. What Kant is arguing is that emotion or desire is a wobbly compass by which to steer our choices because love, pity, generosity are things which depend on the circumstance (or whether I've just had a row with the mother-in-law or eaten something dubious for breakfast).

Moreover, I can act for example out of pity and do something quite immoral, like let off a someone who tells me a sob story about how his little dog has just died. The US public rallied behind President Nixon when he was accused in 1971 of accepting bribes: he went on TV and talked about the gift of a little dog "and you know something? Pat (his wife) really loved that dog".

In order to guard against this possibility of being moved by unreliable emotion, Kant argues that the only pure good is to act out of respect for the moral law, to act out of duty. Schneewind comments:

> *"If merit accrues only when we act from a sense of duty, it seems that human relations must either be unduly chilly or else without moral worth. Did Kant really hold this view? There are passages which suggest he did. He rejects the feeling of love as a proper moral motive (Groundwork 4:399 / 67); he usually treats passions and desires as if their aim is always the agent's own pleasure (Groundwork 4:407/ 75); and at one point he says that the aim of every rational person is to be free from desire (Groundwork 4:428 / 955). In other passages he shows a more humane view (Religion 6:28 / 23; 6:58 / 51). The most plausible alternative to the extreme position is one that allows conditional mixed motives: I may have merit when moved by the motive of pity, say, if I allow pity to operate only on condition that in moving me it leads me to nothing the categorical imperative forbids, and if respect were strong enough to move me were pity to fail." (ed. Guyer, 1992:328)*

THE CATEGORICAL IMPERATIVE

A categorical imperative is an unconditional command. It is always true, everywhere and for all time. The categorical imperative is the central idea in Kant's absolute ethics.

Pure reason wills some end (such as happiness) and also some means to achieve that end (such as a being honest, loyal, or fair); it operates using a method much like Newtonian physics (from a fact such as my feelings or desires to a value such as happiness via a means such as being honest).

Practical reason, argues Kant, "was given to us in order to produce a will which was good not as a means to an end, but good in itself" (Groundwork). So we must test our actions according to a rational process against the standard of the categorical imperative, which is a fixed compass point, like the North Pole, which doesn't change and is derivable a priori. This principle, derived a priori, is then applied synthetically to a real world situation in order to determine what to do.

How can we derive such a principle as the **CATEGORICAL IMPERATIVE** a priori without recourse to arguments from experience, ends (as in Utilitarianism) or emotions (as with Hume's appeal to our natural sympathy or feeling for one another)?

Kant's argument proceeds from certain axioms or starting-points, to a conclusion or maxim. The maxim is known as the categorical imperative whose essential feature is universalisability. Below we discuss this maxim in greater detail: here I wish to derive it simply from certain assumptions, grasped intuitively.

- **ASSUMPTION 1** - We are perfectly rational agents. The structure of our minds is set up as it were in a certain way. We process our perception of the world by principles of rationality: we see cause and effect and time and purpose in things. We are capable of abstracting from our feelings or even the fear of God. This rationality therefore entails freedom.

- **ASSUMPTION 2** - We have freedom of will. We are aware of our freedom intuitively. The desire to follow the moral law within is something we have out of respect for the moral law. We recognise its beauty and validity by intuition (Kant never really proved successfully why we should respect his categorical imperative rather than some other maxim. However, if we accept his two axioms or assumptions, then the conclusion does seem to follow).

- **CONCLUSION** - We will reasonably choose to act only through universal maxims, known as the categorical imperative. Kant believed that the **SUMMUM BONUM**, a state of affairs where goodness and happiness are achieved, can only follow from people consistently and universally (always and everywhere) acting out of duty (rather than feelings or self-interest or some end such as maximising happiness). It's interesting that it is here that God creeps back in, as it were, by the back door, because Kant believed that only in the after-life would a fair distribution of happiness for the virtuous and misery for the selfish be fully achieved.

I knew I should have stayed in Konigsberg!!!
DUTY FREE

The Categorical Imperative

THREE FORMULATIONS

Each way of describing Kant's categorical imperative has another way of describing it, a test we can apply, and implications to understand. Here we try to examine these.

Kant argues that to be moral we need to act on the categorical imperative which we can work out by practical reason alone. A categorical imperative has no exceptions: it is absolute, meaning it is true for everyone, everywhere, whereas a hypothetical imperative usually contains the word **IF**, which implies a reason or a feeling or a situation where the hypothetical might apply (If you're stopped by the police, don't swear!). "You shall not lie", in contrast, is an example of a categorical imperative (no reasons given, no circumstances referred to).

A hypothetical imperative usually contains the word **IF**. This gives a reason, and that reason may be some goal we have (like happiness), some feeling we experience (like compassion or sadness), or a situation we are in ("if you are stopped by the police, don't swear!").

> *"If you want to be happy, you must be honest" (the hypothetical end here is happiness, the means is honesty) contrasts with the categorical "never lie!".*
>
> *"If you want a quiet life, don't retaliate when someone hits you" (the hypothetical end is a quiet life, the means is to walk away from an attacker) contrasts with the categorical "love your enemies!".*

Kant argues that honesty and non-retaliation, if they are seen to be good, are good absolutely irrespective of my desire or my goal. It is an absolute good but (and this is his key contribution to philosophy, perhaps), it is not unreasonable, unlike the dictates of divine command theory which seem to imply I should obey something because God says so, the only "reasonableness" being that I am afraid I might go to hell or displease God, rather than own the action for myself.

Kant is saying effectively that one ought not to lie, regardless of how you feel about it or how you may be tempted to lie. This is entirely reasonable given the assumptions that lie behind his a priori argument, assumptions of rationality and autonomy (freedom of will). This absolute, unyielding, categorical imperative has three formulations worked out deductively and applied synthetically (to the real world).

FIRST FORMULA

The Principle of Law - universalise your actions, implying consistency.

> *"Act only on that maxim by which you can at the same time will that it becomes a universal law."*

Practically, we can test our action with a question: "Am I willing that this action should always be followed by everyone in every situation?" The rules which we then generate, such as "no lying" reflect the rational moral law which can and must have no exceptions. It is absolute and unchanging (like cause and effect or the idea of time).

If we apply the principle of law in a particular situation without exception, we have done our duty. We have acted according to duty alone, from the motive of the "good will".

SECOND FORMULA

The Principle of Ends - universalise your common humanity, implying equality, that every human agent has absolute worth.

> *"Act so that you treat humanity, both in your own person and in the person of every other human being, never merely as a means, but always at the same time as an end."*

Practically, we can test our action with this question: "Am I treating my neighbour as if I was standing in his or her shoes?"

As Raphael (1981:57) puts it: "to treat a man as an end ... is to make his ends your own".

I take into account before I do something:

- The desires
- The feelings
- The interests of the person or people which are directly affected by my action. I do this whilst ignoring my own desires, feelings and interests.

In the first you go into a shop to buy some sweets. Treat the shopkeeper just as a means to an end. In the second, treat the shopkeeper not only as a means to get some sweets, but also as an end in him or herself.

THIRD FORMULA

The principle of autonomy - universalise your idea of shared interests, implying that morality is a shared obligation with some idea of a common good.

> *"Act as if you were, through your maxim a law-making member of a kingdom of ends."*

Practically, we can test our action with this question: "If I was a member of a moral parliament voting according to the national interest, how would I vote?" In other words, I don't need Parliament, the King, my peer group or God to tell me this. As an autonomous, free individual, I can using my own reason work this out for myself.

> *"Each of us has a will that makes laws for itself as if for everyone. Since human beings together legislate the moral law, we form a moral community: a Kingdom of Ends. The Kingdom of Ends is an ideal. It is 'a systematic union of different rational beings through common laws', a republic of all rational beings. It is a community in which freedom is perfectly realised, for its citizens are free both in the sense that they have made their own laws and in the sense that the laws they have made are the laws of freedom - the juridical laws of external freedom and the ethical laws of internal freedom. The Kingdom of Ends is also 'a whole of rational beings as ends in themselves as well as of particular ends which each may set for himself', a system of all good ends. Each citizen takes his own perfection and the happiness of others as an end and treats every other as an end in itself. It is a community engaged in the harmonious and cooperative pursuit of the good." Christine Korsgaard*

And here we are back with Rousseau and his Social Contract, which has recently been developed further by John Rawls in his Theory of Justice. Rawls asks us to imagine we are members of a hypothetical Parliament voting according to two principles of justice:

Each person is to have an equal right to the most extensive basic liberty compatible with a similar liberty for others.

Social and economic inequalities are to be arranged so that:

> *- they are to be of the greatest benefit to the least-advantaged members of society (the difference principle).*
>
> *- offices and positions must be open to everyone under conditions of fair equality of opportunity.*
>
> *(Rawls, 1971, p. 303; revised edition, p. 47):*

In this way we can truly argue that Kantian morality has political implications, and we can see how Kant and Rousseau (with his social contract and general will) walk hand in hand. As Raphael (1994:57) puts it:

> *"It will be seen that the Kantian theory of ethics, like the utilitarian, has political implications. Kantian ethics is in fact the ethics of democracy. It requires liberty (allow everyone to decide for himself), equality (because it requires us to recognise that every human being equally has the power to make moral decisions) and fraternity (think of yourself as a member of a moral community)." Raphael (1987:90)*

This, then, is **A PRIORI** reasoning by the free moral agent, which entails a kind of freedom and dignity for all irrespective of education, class or colour. No wonder Kant is described as producing a kind of Copernican revolution, and Alasdair MacIntyre writes: "For many of us who have never heard of philosophy, let alone Kant, morality is roughly what Kant said it was."

Applying Kant

WHAT MAKES A BAD ACT BAD?

Kant analyses evil as a kind of logical error, or mistake in reasoning. A contradiction is the worst logical error. It would obviously be a contradiction for a rational being to say "Every rational being should do tell the truth, except me." Contradiction of this form is called special pleading.

When rational beings will to do bad things, they want a contradiction: they want everybody else to do the right thing, because that's exactly what makes their wrongdoing possible. For example, the liar wants everyone else to tell the truth; if everyone lied, no one would believe the liar's lie. So the liar in effect is willing a contradiction: "Every rational being should tell the truth, except me." To want the rule to apply to everyone but not to me is a failure of universalisability, the first formulation of the Categorical Imperative.

HOW DOES THE REASONING WORK IN PRACTICE?

Using practical reason, there are two steps to establish a bad act. First, we consider what we intend to do and for what reasons (ie, on which maxim). Second, we consider whether we can will that everyone act on that maxim. If we cannot do so, we shouldn't act on it ourselves. We must find some other maxim, one that passes the test.

Kant thinks there are two kinds of case where we couldn't will that everyone act on the maxim.

Cases in which there simply could not be a world in which everyone acts on the maxim because this would destroy everyone else's ability to follow it (he calls this a contradiction in nature):

> *"Some actions are so constituted that their maxim cannot even be conceived as a universal law of nature without contradiction." (Kant, Groundwork 424)*

Cases where one can conceive of a world in which everyone acts on the maxim, but where I cannot consistently or rationally want to live in such a world. (He calls this a contradiction in will.)

In either kind of case, the maxim will fail the Categorical Imperative test. According to Kant, it would be wrong to act on a maxim of either kind.

Kant uses examples of both kinds.

A contradiction in nature

The maxim: "When I believe myself to be in need to money I shall borrow money and promise to repay it, even though I know that this will never happen."

A person proposes to make a promise he doesn't intend to keep to pay back money in order to meet a need of his own. He must consider whether he could will a world in which everyone is motivated in precisely the same way. Kant claims that he cannot since it is only possible for people to promise in the first place if there is sufficient trust for others to believe that the person promising intends to keep his promise.

But a world (otherwise like our own) in which everyone acted on this maxim would be a world in which such trust will not exist. Therefore it is impossible even to conceive of a world in which everyone acts on this maxim as though by a law of nature; therefore it is wrong to act on this maxim myself.

A contradiction in will

The maxim: "Let each be as happy as heaven wills or as he can make himself; I shall take nothing from him nor even envy him; only I do not care to contribute anything to his welfare or to his assistance in need!"

A person proposes not to help others because it is not in his own interest to do so. He then asks whether he could will a world in which everyone is similarly motivated.

Clearly he can imagine such a world, so this kind of case is different from the first. But can he rationally will that everyone act on this maxim as though by a law of nature? It seems he cannot, because in willing that he act on the maxim, he is willing that his own interest be promoted, but in willing that everyone act on the maxim, he is willing that his own interest not be promoted. Thus his will is in conflict with itself.

> *"Since many a situation might arise in which the man needed love and sympathy from others, and in which, by such a law of nature sprung from his own will, he would rob himself of all hope of the help he wants for himself." (Groundwork, 423)*

So a wrong action is one that creates a contradiction in nature or will.

Are the following examples a contradiction in nature or will?

1. I decide to commit suicide.
2. I play my music very loudly at 3am.
3. I borrow money with the intention of never repaying it.
4. I never buy the first round of drinks.
5. I visit my old mother in a nursing home once a year.
6. I am the only class member consistently five minutes late.

TELLING THE TRUTH - THE STRANGE CASE OF THE INQUIRING MURDERER

The strange case of the inquiring murderer is contained in an essay Kant wrote as a much older man, called "On a Supposed Right to lie from Altruistic Motives". In it he asks us to consider the situation of a murderer just outside our friend's house. The murderer asks us "is your friend inside?" How do we answer?

If I say "yes" there is a danger the murderer will go straight in and kill my friend. The speech bubble might read "Yes, one ought never to lie!"

If I say "no", Kant argues that it is possible that my friend has slipped out, and the murderer will find him in the park and kill him, and if that's the case, "you might justly be accused of causing his death", and Kant concludes:

> *"Therefore, whoever tells a lie, however well intentioned he might be, must answer for the consequences, however unforeseeable they were, and pay the penalty for them ... to be truthful (honest) in all deliberations, therefore, is a sacred and absolutely commanding decree of reason, limited to no expediency."*
> *Immanuel Kant*

How might Kant have reached this counter-intuitive answer?

Well, perhaps he saw that if all of us absolutely and always followed the categorical imperative, exercising the "good will" and universalising our actions, then the summum bonum of a society which respected the moral "ought" and put it above feelings might just be realisable on this earth, and so we wouldn't need the back door argument that we need God to put things straight and reward the virtuous in the next life.

If so, our poor friend has been sacrificed, as in the utilitarian position, for the greater good, and a teleological end. But do we really have to present the situation in such a stark way?

However, we can put some other things in speech bubbles which temper this truth-telling with wisdom. Rather than just say "yes" or "no", it is no lie to ask a question for example."Why do you want to know?" is not a lie, nor is a question necessarily implying we know the answer. "What makes you think I've got the faintest idea?"

We might also deter the murderer by saying something like: "You lay a finger on my friend and I'll kill you!" or even "Calm down, killing never solved anything!"

None of these answers breaks the categorical imperative (which doesn't forbid us being evasive, aggressive or even vague!). Moreover, there is a basic logical flaw in this argument of Kant. If I am responsible for the unintended consequences of telling a lie, I must also be responsible for the unintended consequences of telling the truth.

Rachels (1994) goes further. He argues that consistency does not necessarily imply that we must accept rules without exceptions. In other words, the rules do not have to be absolute. We could have a rule "lying is wrong, unless we meet a situation where anyone who is rational would have to lie, such as saving a life". If we can conceive of a rational person, acting out of duty, admitting the same exception to the rule, then we can universalise a rule-with-exceptions built in.

> *"All that is required by Kant's basic idea is that when we violate a rule, we do so for a reason that we would be willing for anyone to accept, were they in our position." (Rachels, 1994:126)*

www.beingandtim.com

Deontological Non-Absolutism: WD Ross

WD Ross (1877-1971) believed in the **INTRINSIC** goodness of pleasure and happiness but (a bit like the rule utilitarian Mill) that this happiness is best served by obeying duties, such as our duty to tell the truth. But he also felt that there was a problem about conflicting duties, such as the example of the crazy axe murderer where our duty to save our friend's life conflicts with our duty to tell the truth.

If duties conflict, how can duties be unconditional, allowing no exceptions? Ross argued that Kantian duties should not be taken as absolute duties but as **PRIMA FACIE DUTIES** (meaning "at first sight"). These are duties we know by intuition, but they can be overriden.

Henry Sidgwick defines an intuition as an "immediate judgement" we make as a kind of perception. We make it without reflection. But Sidgwick also discusses a second meaning, one which involves discussion and reflection "to remove inconsistencies and prevent conflict". (p. 101)

To Ross, we have an a priori perception of what is right in a certain situation, but this comes not from viewing consequences, but because of some duty which the action fulfils, such as keeping a promise.

Then when duties conflict, a second, more reflective process of intuition kicks in: we know intuitively which duty has precedence over the other. So duties can tell us what we ought to do "nothing else considered" (at first sight), but they can't tell us what to do "all things considered" (as it were, at second sight).

Is this one way to escape the problem of conflicting duties?

Ross suggests six types of duty:

1. **DUTIES OF FIDELITY AND REPARATION** - The duty to keep promises, for example.

2. **DUTIES OF GRATITUDE** - To return favours done to us such as lending something to a neighbour who has just lent us some tools.

3. **DUTIES OF JUSTICE** - "Some rest on the fact or possibility of a distribution of pleasure or happiness which is not in accordance with the merit of the persons concerned; in such cases there arises a duty to upset or prevent such a distribution." (WD Ross)

4. **DUTIES OF BENEFICENCE** - The duty to maximise the good, to improve someone's condition or give them pleasure or happiness, for example, helping a stranger whose car has broken down.

5. **DUTIES OF SELF IMPROVEMENT** - If we can better our own character or circumstances we should do so, for example, by keeping fit.

6. **DUTIES OF NONMALEFICENCE** - "Duties that can be summed up as not harming others" (WD Ross), such as avoiding cruel words or deliberate injury.

Ross concludes:

"We have no more direct access to the facts about rightness and goodness and about what things are right or good, than by

thinking about them; the moral convictions of thoughtful and well educated people are the data of ethics." (The Right and the Good, 1930)

We can question Ross on two grounds. Is this list complete? What about the duty of non-parasitism - of not being a free rider on everyone else's tax revenue, for example. Ross might counter that this is included in the idea of justice. But this raises an interesting point: does my idea of justice agree with yours? If they disagree, why do they do so, and who is to judge between us? After all, many of us avoid tax by paying the plumber in cash, but still enjoy the social services we thereby avoid paying for.

And many people have no qualms about inflating their insurance claims, or claiming a breakage was actually damaged goods which demand a refund. In this way we become parasites on everyone else's honesty, otherwise everyone would suffer higher insurance premiums.

Secondly Ross' argument begs the question: where do intuitions come from? Ross believes we know our duties because they are self-evident, like the truth that 2+2=4. But we can counter: we need to learn that two plus two equals four, and this involves understanding the idea of number. Presumably a tribesman in the Amazon would have no such concept. Are intuitions really self-evident? Or are they another form of relativist cultural construct?

If Ross is wrong about this, then we need to establish the truth of morality by argument, not by intuition, and perhaps if we fail to have this debate we fail in another type of duty - the duty to integrity, to own truth for ourselves.

KANT'S STRENGTHS AND WEAKNESSES

Strengths

- **CLARITY** - Kant's categorical imperative generates absolute rules, with no exceptions, which are easy to follow. Kant argued that rational beings understand what they should do (discounting desires and feelings), out of duty alone, and so apply the categorical imperative consistently in similar circumstances to give us rules eg "do not steal", "do not lie", "help a friend in need".

"Everyone who is ideally rational will legislate the same universal principles." Pojman (2002:147)

"Hypothetical oughts are possible because we have desires, categorical oughts are possible because we have reason." Rachels (2007:119)

- **DIGNITY/EQUALITY** - The value of human beings is absolute, Kant said "beyond all price", and all of us must try to further the interests of others and treat them with respect.

"We have unconditional worth and so must treat all value-givers as valuable in themselves." Pojman (2002:145)

"Humans have intrinsic worth, ie dignity, because they are rational agents - that is, free agents ... guiding their conduct by reason." Rachels (2007:129)

- **CONSISTENCY** - We are consistent in how we apply rules (we don't exempt ourselves or others), and how we treat people (as "ends" with dignity and rights).

"Moral reasons, if they are valid at all, are binding on all people at all times ... it implies that a person cannot regard himself as special, from a moral point of view ... that his interests are more important than others." Rachels (2007:126)

Weaknesses

- **HARSHNESS/RETRIBUTION** - Kant believed in an eye for an eye and hanging murderers: "an evil deed draws punishment on itself". Respecting people's rationality means holding them accountable for their actions. If someone is kind to you be kind back ... and vice versa. Retribution (correct payment for wrongdoing) is good as it respects dignity and consistency.

"Reward and punishment are the natural expression of gratitude and resentment." Rachels (2007:137)

- **RIGIDITY** - Kant gave the example of the murderer who asks: "is your friend hiding in the house?" and argued "to be honest in all deliberations is a sacred and absolutely commanding decree of reason ... whoever tells a lie must answer for the consequences". But aren't we responsible too when we tell the truth and our friend is killed? Kant believed that lying could not be adopted universally as a good thing because it would be self-defeating: trust would go and we would hurt each other.

- **SPECIESISM** - Because we are differentiated from animals by our reason, and it is our reason that gives us dignity, it follows, argued Kant, that animals cannot be given the same dignity and rights.

"As far as animals are concerned, we have no direct duties. Animals ... are there merely as means to an end. That end is man." Kant, Lectures on Ethics

QUOTES - WHAT THE ACADEMICS SAY ABOUT KANT

1. *"Kant places the stern ethics of duty at the heart of the moral life." (Robert Arrington, 1980:264)*

2. *"The typical examples of alleged Categorical Imperatives given by Kant tell us what not to do; not to break promises, tell lies, commit suicide, and so on. But as to what activities we ought to engage in, what ends we should pursue, the Categorical Imperative seems strangely silent." (Alasdair MacIntyre, 1967)*

3. *"His own rigoristic convictions on the subject of lying were so intense that it never occurred to him that a lie could be relevantly described as anything but just a lie (eg 'a lie in such-and-such circumstances'). His rule about universalisable maxims is useless without stipulations as to what shall count as a relevant description of an action with a view to constructing a maxim about it." (Elisabeth Anscombe, Philosophy, 1958:2)*

4. *"The Categorical Imperative will really not do as an explanation of where ethics comes from. Its weakness lies in this separation of reason from all other human propensities." (Mary Warnock, 1998)*

5. *"Given Kant's Newtonian model of the physical world, a strong claim about the freedom of the will raises problems. Our bodies as physical objects are subject to Newton's laws of motion. If they are moved by our natural desires, this is unproblematic, because desires themselves arise in accordance with deterministic laws (as yet undiscovered). Morality, however, requires the possibility of*

action from a non-empirical motive. We never know if real moral merit is attained, but if it is, the motive of respect for the moral law must move us to bodily action, regardless of the strength of our desires. Is this possible?" (JB Schneewind, ed. Guyer, 1992)

6. *"The difference between a value and a rule is that it makes sense to maximize a value - to increase it as much as possible - whereas we can only comply with a rule. So if I value happiness, I can choose between acts that will lead to there being more or less happiness in the world, but if I accept the rule that I should never kill an innocent human being, I can only comply with the rule, or break it ... Consider this question: should I be ready to kill an innocent human being if, by doing so, I can somehow prevent the killing of several other innocent human beings? An affirmative answer suggests that you regard the reduction of killing of innocent human beings as a value; only a negative answer is consistent with treating the non-killing of innocent human beings as a rule." (P Singer, 1994:11)*

7. *The trouble with Kant, according to Anthony Quinton (Philosophy 72 [1997], 5-18), is that he does not take empirical experience to have any significant role to play in our knowledge of the world. The world we know is constituted through the imposition of a priori forms - space, time, substance and cause - on a "wholly passive sensory raw material". This sensory material does not guide the manner in which the a priori forms are imposed in any way, so that the imposition is "entirely arbitrary". Thus, Kant's "account of the matter allows for an indefinitely large number of orders in which our successive manifolds of*

sensation could be arranged. None of these ways of distinguishing what there is and occurs from what I merely think is and occurs has any priority or superiority to any of the others." (Quinton, 17-18)

KEY TERMS

- **DEONTOLOGICAL**
- **TELEOLOGICAL**
- **CATEGORICAL**
- **HYPOTHETICAL**
- **IMPERATIVE**
- **UNIVERSALISABILITY**
- **FORMULA OF ENDS**
- **AUTONOMY**
- **NOUMENAL REALM**
- **PHENOMENAL REALM**
- **A PRIORI**
- **A POSTERIORI**
- **CONTRADICTION IN WILL**
- **CONTRADICTION IN NATURE**
- **SUMMUM BONUM**
- **THREE POSTULATES**

SELF-TEST QUESTIONS

1. Explain why the assumption of autonomy is important to Kantian ethics.
2. What did Kant mean by suggesting that the moral law existed as an a priori category of the mind?
3. Explain the difference between a hypothetical and a categorical imperative.
4. Why is Kantian ethics sometimes described as the cold-hearted ethics of duty (Arrington)?
5. Explain why Kant believed moral imperatives applied to everyone (they are universal).
6. Explain what Kant meant when he said you should never treat people just as a means to an end (the second formulation or formula of ends).
7. What is the difference between a contradiction in will, and a contradiction in nature? Give examples.
8. Why did Kant believe breaking promises is always wrong?
9. How might Kant's view be criticised that the only good thing is the good will? What about the feeling of moral disgust?
10. How important is God for Kantian ethics?

FURTHER READING

- **GROSCH, P & LARGE, W** - Kant's Categorical Imperative Dialogue 5 (November 1994)
- **O'NEILL, O** - in Singer ed., A Companion to Ethics, Blackwell (1993) Ch 14
- **POJMAN, L** - Ethics, Discovering Right and Wrong, Thomas Wadsworth (2006) Ch 7
- **RACHELS, J** - The Elements of Moral Philosophy, McGraw-Hill (1993) Ch 9&10
- **RAPHAEL, DD** - Moral Philosophy (second edition), Opus (1994) Ch 6
- **SCHNEEWIND, JB** - in Guyer ed., The Cambridge Companion to Kant, CUP (1992) Ch 10
- **SCRUTON, R** - Kant, OUP (2001) Ch 5
- **QUINTON, A** - The Trouble with Kant, Philosophy 72 (1997) 5-18

Natural Law

"The semi-official philosophy of the Roman Catholic Church to this day." Peter Singer

"Natural Law is the sharing in the eternal law by intelligent creatures." Aquinas

Natural Law works on the assumption that we have, within our own nature, a guide to what is good for us. If we follow that we flourish (Greek: "eudaimonia"). Natural Law assumes there is an unchanging normative order that is a part of the natural world. Many assume it means that "what is natural is good"; instead, we should define natural here as "fulfilling its true purpose".

INTRODUCTION

When a child says "it's not fair", when you or I watch the film Hotel Rwanda or Schindler's List and think "this genocide is absolute evil" we are providing evidence that there may be such a thing as a "natural law": a view of the world which all of us share by our very natures which informs our view of right and wrong.

CS Lewis (1964) explained it this way:

> *"According to the religious view, what is behind the universe is more like a mind than anything else we know ... it is conscious, and has purposes, and prefers one thing to another. And on this view it made the universe, partly for purposes we do not know, but partly in order to produce creatures like itself ... having minds ... There is a something which is directing the universe, and which appears to me as a law urging me to do right." (Mere Christianity, pp. 16, 19, 33)*

There are a number of features of Natural Law theory:

- **DEONTOLOGICAL** because it produces rules and duties. Strictly speaking, it's a deontological theory which comes out of a teleological worldview, the Greek view that everything has a purpose (telos) and the purpose of human beings is distinctive and rational.

- **ABSOLUTE** because the natural law is absolute and unchanging, "a sharing in the eternal law by intelligent creatures". (Aquinas)

- **NORMATIVE** because natural law creates norms or values which are inherent in the natural order, accessed by our reason.

Many Protestant theologians do not accept Natural Law theory (I shall quote some later, but Karl Barth and Roald Niebuhr are certainly two) because their key assumption is that all human beings "fall short of the glory of God" (Romans 3:23) and are born into sin.

Synderesis: 'each precious child, born with the desire to do good, and avoid evil'

The Nature of Aquinas' Teleology

THE SYNDERESIS PRINCIPLE

Aquinas calls synderesis "the first principle of the natural law", that humans have a natural desire to "do good and avoid evil". Aquinas needs this starting point to create a syllogism or logical argument from a first premise (or assumption he makes, that we are all good by nature). It is this assumption that Protestant christians tend to reject, believing us to be born in a fallen, sinful state.

The argument goes like this:

All human beings naturally pursue good and avoid evil: a natural habit.

We can observe a posteriori (by sense experience) the ends that rational people pursue.

So these rational ends must be good (the primary precepts).

THE LOGIC OF NATURAL LAW

1. Our human nature is so ordered that we naturally "do good and avoid evil", the synderesis principle. We have a priori knowledge of the goodness of the primary precepts.

2. The good is defined as the ends which we rationally pursue.

3. There are five general, universal, absolute ends, the primary precepts.

4. These general ends are then applied, using practical wisdom to situations. These "proximate conclusions" are the secondary precepts of the natural law, and are relative and may change.

5. There are four laws: the eternal law of God, the divine law of revelation, the human law which we pass, and the natural law which we follow by a priori knowledge and then observe in the a posteriori world of experience and choice.

6. We may fail to act on the natural law, but we cannot knowingly break it because of the synderesis principle. So we believe we do good even though in fact we may be doing evil. These are apparent goods.

7. Our intention is important. The intention (to save a life) is an interior good, and should correspond to the exterior good of an action.

8. The doctrine of double effect states that if the primary intention is to do good (save a mother's life) and a secondary bad consequence happens (a foetus dies), there is no moral blame.

9. The ultimate end is eudaimonia, a flourishing life where well-being is maximised and excellence of character achieved.

10. For Aquinas, this was only perfectly achieved in heaven because the goal is to be with God and like God.

ANCIENT ROOTS IN GREEK TELEOLOGY

> *"Thomas was convinced that the teleological ethics of Aristotle was, in general, sound, and that the Greek philosopher's way of thinking provided a philosophical backbone ... for a Christian ethics." Francis Coplestone*

Aristotle distinguished four causes or explanations of why things are as they are:

MATERIAL - What things come from, eg the material cause of a sculpture is a block of marble.

FORMAL - The plans, what things are to be - the idea in the mind of the sculptor.

EFFICIENT - "The source of the primary principle of change or stability" - the artist working on his work.

FINAL - Something fulfilling its purpose or telos - the end result, the completed sculpture.

Take sex, for example. With sex the efficient cause is a statement of fact or a description. If we ask why people have sex, we might talk about physical attraction, psychological needs or bodily pleasure. The final cause or end is a matter of intent - what was God's purpose behind sex? The final cause assumes a rational mind behind creation, and as such moves from descriptive ethics (saying what is there) to normative ethics (statements about what should or should not be the case). These final causes (or goods or purposes) Aquinas calls **OBJECTS OF THE WILL** (think of objectives).

Take the example of a soldier who shoots someone. Was he a "good shot"? The efficient cause deals with the set of events around the shooting - did he aim well, was the shot accurate, did the target die? These are descriptive points, and clearly don't tell us about the morality of the shooting. When we look into this area - was it right to kill? - we are evaluating his intent, and are asking about the final cause, the end or object of the action.

We can then look at whether that cause is consistent with God's design for human beings. We may decide that killing innocent people goes against God's design for us, so it is always wrong to kill innocent people, or that in time of war or for reasons of self-defence, killing is justified. It's for this reason that Ralph McInery comments in his excellent introduction to Aquinas:

> *"It is because the ultimate end is implicit in every human action that Thomas can hold that natural law is valid for all men at all times." Ralph McInery (1997:47)*

But here we encounter a problem: we might all differ not just in the list of **ACTIVITIES WHICH LEAD TO THE ULTIMATE GOOD** (victory, health, growth), but also **WHAT THE INTERMEDIATE GOOD MIGHT**

BE (trained troops, innoculation, low inflation). For example, some might argue that nuclear bombs, diet and low unemployment were more appropriate intermediate goods.

Take sex, for example. As an activity is its final good (what it aims at) procreation, or is it bonding, or is it both?

Sex ---?---> right time in the cycle ----- ?------> babies?

Sex ---?---> fun and often -----?------> bonding?

And there's a second problem: just because every road stops somewhere (every activity has an end), it doesn't follow that every road ends up in the same place (not every activity ends up in causing us to flourish as human beings). Put another way, there's good sex and bad sex (even if the end is babies; sex can be exploitative, or violent or selfish).

Has Aristotle in fact ended up on a roundabout, producing a classic **CIRCULAR ARGUMENT**: every activity aims at some good; I am aiming at something now; therefore what I'm aiming at must be something good.

APPLICATION OF THE TELEOLOGICAL WORLDVIEW TO ETHICS

Aristotle argued the idea of final and efficient cause applied also to ethics. Aristotle begins his Nichomachean Ethics by arguing:

> *"Every art and every investigation, every action and pursuit, is thought to aim at some good: and for this reason the good has rightly been declared as that to which all things aim."*

At first reading this seems a curious thing to argue. If I am aiming to make a lot of money, or have sexual relations with many different people, these things are clearly reasonable aims for many people today, but are they good? Doesn't Aristotle beg the very question he is trying to answer (namely, what exactly should we be aiming at)? Let's unpack his ideas more closely:

- Every plant or animal has a distinct purpose and we are all interconnected (in the words of the Lion King) "in the great circle of life". Bees pollinate flowers; fish are food for other fish; animals depend on one another for survival, and humans?
- Human beings have a special potential: to use their reason (**PHRONESIS** or practical wisdom) to flourish.By a process of observation of the natural world humans can understand the composition and workings of this world, but also, to understand what we mean by "the good".
- There is an ultimate purpose, which is flourishing or happiness, translated from the Greek word **EUDAIMONIA**. This word implies an organic process of growth of character which

continues throughout our lives. It is a very different idea from the secular concept of happiness today.

- Character is crucial to discovering this end or telos. In the formation of character we need to concentrate on the virtues and particularly the mean between the vice of deficiency (those things that stop us realising our potential) and the vice of excess. This prudential mean is the key to the moral life (so courage is a mean virtue between cowardice and rashness).

So by focusing on the efficient and final causes not only can we see that everything has a purpose but also its supreme good is to be found when it fulfils that purpose.

Here are some examples of supreme goods in the table below:

PURPOSE	**SUPREME GOOD**
Bees	Honey
Flowers	Beauty and scent
Volcanos	Rock formation from lava
Cows	Milk and beef
Humans	Rationality

Wildlife documentaries show us examples of life in the natural world. We find that the goodness of nature is ambiguous: it is often cruel, capricious, and even senseless. Does this suggest to us that natural purpose isn't quite as clearly good as Aquinas suggests?

Reason and Ultimate Purpose

AQUINAS AND ARISTOTLE, EUDAIMONIA AND GOD

For Aquinas, Aristotle's efficient and final causes meant people fulfilling their perfection - this is attaining the highest level of existence that puts them in touch with God and brings to completion God's plans for them. The word for this ultimate goal is **EUDAIMONIA** or human flourishing.

THE FALL OF TOLEDO 1085

In 1085 the Christian armies swept south through Spain reconquering parts lost to the Muslim armies 150 years before, and captured the city of Toledo in central Castile. Toledo had become famous for the happy Convivencia, living together of three major religions (Jews, Christians, and Muslims) which was maintained until 1492 when expulsions of Jews began. There they found manuscripts in Aramaic of the entire known works of Aristotle, including his philosophy and ethics. Soon Toledo became a translation centre for these treasures preserved by Islam. As Aristotle's ideas began to permeate Europe, Aquinas sought to reconcile the Greek worldview with Christianity. His great work **SUMMA THEOLOGICA** (often written **ST** for short) is the fruit of this synthesis.

Aristotle felt the final end was to live a happy life in this world but Aquinas extended this to see living a good life now as a step to eternal life with God.

For Aquinas nothing in this world can satisfy human desires - worldly goods leave a person incomplete. Whatever a persons' accomplishments or wealth they have not completed their inner sense or purpose .

> *"Because in all things whatsoever there is an appetite for completion, the final end to which each moves makes its own perfect and fulfilling good."*

The final end for humans is God:

> *"Our ultimate end is unrelated good, namely God, who alone can fill our will to the brim because of infinite goodness."*
> *Aquinas (CT Ch 101)*

In this life we live in preparation for the next - human reason provides the guide - although this cannot grasp everything about God it enables a man to live the life ordained for him by God. The end point is that all of us become assimilated into the divine goodness. (CT Chapter 101)

This is essentially Aristotelian - humans are different from other animals as they have reason. The proper life for them is to guide their life by their reason. Reason is able to discern the ethical principles which God intends us to live our lives by. By living a life of reason we are able to fulfil our potential and move closer to our final end - God. It is our reason that connects us with Natural Law.

HUMAN BEHAVIOUR AND REASON

Aquinas argued that humans act to fulfil a purpose (telos): they act to attain goals and their desires move them to ends that will satisfy these desires. Although we might try to suppress this natural goodness, it breaks out in unexpected ways.

Aquinas thought there were three types of desire (sometimes called appetites or inclinations) which influence our behaviour:

NATURAL INCLINATIONS - Shared with other creatures, such as reproduction and the desire to preservation of life.

SENSE APPETITES - Love, desire for pleasure, fear and desire to avoid pain.

RATIONAL APPETITES - To do good as suggested by reason. This is the thing that set humans apart from animals and the one over which we exercise control. We express this nature when our senses are guided by reason.

> *"Whatever is contrary to the order of reason is contrary to the nature of human beings..the good of the human being is being in agreement with reason." (Aquinas ST I II Q72)*

So laws of the state become "an ordinance of reason for the common good, promulgated by him who has the care of the community". These take us some way to achieving these goals by helping us flourish in society. The aim of society is to align state law with the natural law to build a flourishing community.

But there is another law:

"Granted that the world is ruled by Divine Providence ... that the whole community of the universe is governed by Divine Reason. Wherefore the very idea of the government of things in God the Ruler of the universe, has the nature of a law. And since the Divine Reason's conception of things is not subject to time but is eternal ... therefore it is that this kind of law must be called eternal ... the eternal concept of the Divine law bears the character of an eternal law, in so far as it is ordained by God to the government of things foreknown by Him." (Aquinas ST I II Q91 A2)

A human cannot grasp the mind of God but God's laws have been incorporated into human nature, which therefore reflects them. The precepts of Natural Law conform to the basic rational tendencies of human beings. By reflecting on what God wants us to do we become aware of the human essence or idea with which God made us, and come to appreciate God's eternal law. Values exist objectively, independent of human reason, in the eternal law of God, their ultimate source, but we deduce human values from reflecting on our own natures and our place in the universe.

"Now this sharing in the Eternal Law by intelligent creatures is what we call Natural Law." (Aquinas ST I II Q91)

Not all God's laws are available by reason: some are imposed upon Christians by God - this is Divine Law, as found in the Bible.

THE FOUR LAWS - AN ANALOGY MIGHT HELP

Imagine you receive a new BMW Mini for your birthday. You find that the owner's manual is missing, so you decide to ask a mechanic friend, who's wise with cars, to come round and sort out for you what everything does. What does he do? He looks under the bonnet, tries the various switches, tests the brakes and then shows you how the car works. By observation he has worked out what would be in the manual. The more skilled he is as a mechanic the better his observations will be.

The **ETERNAL LAW** is the original idea in God's mind.

The **DIVINE LAW** is like an old, incomplete manual (the Bible has gaps and errors in it).

The **NATURAL LAW** is what the mechanic both observes and knows innately (so we work out what the instructions are, and the more skilled we are, the better the manual from observation will be, but the natural law in the **SYNDERESIS** rule is also innate).

The **HUMAN LAW** would be the mechanic's own version of the manual using his practical wisdom or **PHRONESIS** to work out the purpose of the parts.

SUMMARY - REASON, NATURE AND GOAL

Using the diagram below, try to understand the relation between reason, our true nature and the goal of **EUDAIMONIA** in Aquinas' thinking. Notice that phronesis is a virtue or skill we must learn in order to be self-fulfilled. This skill is best thought of as "right judgement" or "appropriate decision-making". The skill makes sense according to the (relativistic) goal of flourishing agreed on by society or a social group.

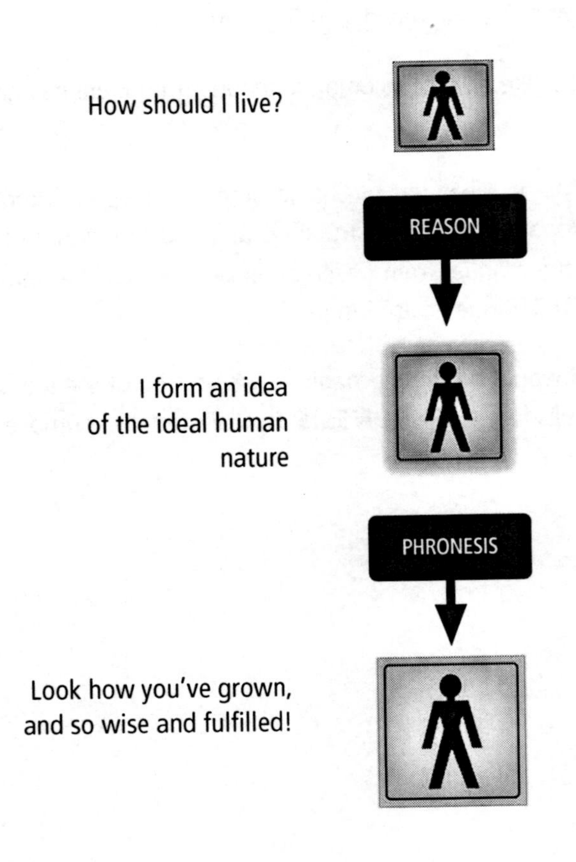

Developing Natural Law

PRIMARY AND SECONDARY PRECEPTS

- What are these natural laws which reflect God's eternal laws? Through synderesis (literally "knowing together") we have an innate, intuitive grasp of God's law. Aquinas calls synderesis "the habitual knowledge of first principles", meaning they are grasped a priori, before experience.

"The first principle of practical reason is one founded on the idea of good, that 'good is that which all things seek after'. Hence this is the first precept of law, that 'good is to be done and pursued, and evil is to be avoided'. All other precepts of the natural law are based upon this so that whatever the practical reason naturally apprehends as man's good (or evil) belongs to the precepts of the natural law as something to be done or avoided.

Since, however, good has the nature of an end, and evil, the nature of a contrary, hence it is that all those things to which man has a natural inclination, are naturally understood by our reason as being good, and consequently as objects of pursuit. So according to the order of natural inclinations, is the order of the precepts of the natural law. Because in man there is first of all an inclination to good in accordance with the nature which he has in common with all substances: inasmuch as every substance seeks the preservation of its own being." (Aquinas ST I II Q94)

The first principle of the natural law is to "do good and avoid evil" and from this flows Aquinas' Primary Precepts which are self-evident, always true and to be obeyed as absolutes - this gives Natural Law its absolute quality. Goodness has the "nature of an end" - the good is what rational people pursue. These ends correspond to "the order of natural inclinations" - goodness is defined by the ends we by nature want. The first natural inclination everyone has, Aquinas argues, is to act according to reason.

These universal rational precepts are as follows:

- **P**reserve life and protect health
- **O**rdered Society
- **W**orship God
- **E**ducation
- **R**eproduction

The first letters of the primary precepts spell **POWER**. If we can find examples in our own experience this might suggest there is indeed a shared rational nature and desire to "do good and avoid evil".

Thomas Aquinas describes the primary precepts as absolute and unchanging. Given that "worship God" is now interpreted by the Roman Catholic Church as "contemplation of beauty" (Veritatis Splendor,1995), it seems that even the **PRIMARY PRECEPTS** are liable to readjustment. God and a beautiful picture are connected by the openness to the numinous in human nature - the feeling of awe which is close to worship.

SECONDARY PRECEPTS are commands which are developed from the general primary precepts and make these commands clearer and more specific. Aquinas calls them "proximate conclusions". These hold in most circumstances but they are not completely absolute because humans may make an error in reasoning and they require knowledge of the human condition to be able to apply the primary precept. Like Aristotle, Aquinas emphasises the need for "perception" - the individual must judge whether or not the precept applies. Aquinas' Natural Law theory is not as absolute as it first appears. Aquinas says:

> *"A change in the natural law may be understood in two ways. First, by way of addition. In this sense nothing hinders the natural law from being changed: since many things for the benefit of human life have been added over and above the natural law, both by the Divine law and by human laws.*
>
> *"Secondly, a change in the natural law may be understood by way of subtraction, so that what previously was according to the natural law, ceases to be so. In this sense, the natural law is altogether unchangeable in its first principles: but in its secondary principles, which, as we have said, are certain detailed proximate conclusions drawn from the first principles, the natural law is not changed so that what it prescribes be not right in most cases. But*

it may be changed in some particular cases of rare occurrence, through some special causes hindering the observance of such precepts".
(Aquinas ST I.II Q94 A5)

A MODERN EXAMPLE OF A RARE OCCURRENCE

In 1972 an aeroplane carrying a Uruguayan rugby team crashed in the Andes. After 72 days without rescue two of them stumbled upon a Chilean shepherd and the survivors were saved. But they had only survived for ten weeks by eating human flesh.

Roberto Canessa recently explained: "I think the greatest sadness I ever felt was when I had to eat a dead body. I would ask myself: is it worth doing this? And it was in order to live and preserve life, which is exactly what I would have liked for myself had I been lying dead on the floor."

The secondary application of the primary precept "Preserve Life" changed in these unusual and tragic circumstances, and it became morally right to eat a human carcass.

MODERN NATURAL LAW INTERPRETATION

Peter Singer has described Natural Law theory as "the semi-official philosophy of the Roman Catholic Church to this day". Natural Law reasoning appears in many papal encyclicals (meaning "circulated letters"). Below is an extract from Veritatis Splendor (1995, meaning "the splendour of truth"). Note carefully the changes that have been made to the primary precepts listed above (**POWER**), which perhaps suggest that the primary precepts are not as absolute as Aquinas thought.

> *"Precisely because of this 'truth' the natural law involves universality. Inasmuch as it is inscribed in the rational nature of the person, it makes itself felt to all beings endowed with reason and living in history. In order to perfect himself in his specific order, the person must do good and avoid evil, be concerned for the transmission and preservation of life, refine and develop the riches of the material world, cultivate social life, seek truth, practise good and contemplate beauty." (Veritatis Splendor paragraph 51)*

The encyclical goes on to describe the essentially teleological nature of Natural Law - reminding us again to describe it as a deontological theory coming from a Greek teleological worldview.

> *"Consequently the moral life has an essential 'teleological' character, since it consists in the deliberate ordering of human acts to God, the supreme good and ultimate end (telos) of man." (Veritatis Splendor, John Paul II, 1995, paragraph 73)*

The papal encyclical of John Paul II, Veritatis Splendor (1995), goes on to argue for the intrinsic nature of this goodness.

> *"Reason attests that there are objects of the human act which are by their nature 'incapable of being ordered' to God, because they radically contradict the good of the person made in his image. These are the acts which, in the Church's moral tradition, have been termed 'intrinsically evil' (intrinsece malum): they are such always and per se, in other words, on account of their very object,*

and quite apart from the ulterior intentions of the one acting and the circumstances."

Consequently, the Roman Catholic Church re-emphasises in this document the teleological nature of Natural Law: that goodness comes from the goal or object of the action, and that objects or goals are defined by the rational nature of human beings as designed by God.

The Catholic Church doesn't deny influence on morality exercised by circumstances and especially by intentions, but argues for intrinsic goodness - that "there exist acts which per se and in themselves, independently of circumstances, are always seriously wrong by reason of their object".

The Second Vatican Council itself, in discussing the respect due to the human person, gives a number of examples of such acts:

> *"Whatever is hostile to life itself, such as any kind of homicide, genocide, abortion, euthanasia and voluntary suicide; whatever violates the integrity of the human person, such as mutilation, physical and mental torture and attempts to coerce the spirit; whatever is offensive to human dignity, such as subhuman living conditions, arbitrary imprisonment, deportation, slavery, prostitution and trafficking in women and children; degrading conditions of work which treat labourers as mere instruments of profit, and not as free responsible persons: all these and the like are a disgrace, and so long as they infect human civilisation they contaminate those who inflict them more than those who suffer injustice, and they are a negation of the honour due to the Creator."*

Applying Natural Law

MORAL WEAKNESS - REAL AND APPARENT GOODS

Like Aristotle, Aquinas did not believe that a human being could deliberately do evil. If they did, this would disprove the **SYNDERESIS** principle, that we by nature "do good and avoid evil". Aquinas believed that people chose either real or apparent goods. A real good is something that is good according to natural law, an **APPARENT GOOD** is a mistake: you wanted to do good but you ended up not doing so. According to Aquinas Hitler would be aiming for an apparent good in his policy of mass murder.

Aquinas argued that people "seek whatever they seek under the formality of goodness". (ST I II Q16 Ac) Everyone desires to achieve their own perfection - pursues **EUDAIMONIA** - but not everyone agrees about how this may be realised. Let's call this individual judgement desire 1.

Some are led astray by passions, others by false reasoning, but all believe they are pursuing the good. The "formality of goodness" is the logical result of everyone believing they are pursuing the best (even though some are mistaken).

In this way although people may not deliberately do evil, they can pursue apparent goods and so be guilty of sin or of an "evil will", because in the end there is an objective morality given by natural law.

The objective morality we can call desire 2, or what is called the objective or **FORMAL IDEA** of goodness.

Only when desire 1 (what I want) = desire 2 (what natural law says we should want) do we flourish.

> *"It happens sometimes that the universal principle is destroyed by a passion: thus to someone swayed by sex, when overcome thereby, the object of the desire seems good, although opposed to the universal judgement of reason ... so in order that he be rightly disposed of the ends, he needs to be perfected by certain habits ... this is done by moral virtue, consequently, the right reason about things to be done, phronesis, requires man to have moral virtue." (Thomas Aquinas ST I II Q58)*

APPLICATION TO SEXUAL ETHICS

We can apply natural law theory to the issue: is contraception morally right? The Roman Catholic Church suggests it is always a grave sin to interfere with the natural purpose of sex, which is reproduction.

> *"Every marital act must of necessity retain its intrinsic relationship to the procreation of human life ... this is a result of laws written into the actual nature of man and woman ... our contemporaries are particularly capable of seeing this teaching is in harmony with human reason ... it is never lawful, even for the gravest reasons, to do evil that good may come of it." (Humanae Vitae, 1967)*

What happens if you disobey the natural law on reproduction? If the final end is to flourish, natural law theory suggests that if you, for example, have sex merely for pleasure the you reduce your own potential for human flourishing and happiness. There is something fundamentally irrational about having sex just for pleasure.

For further research: in the Second Vatican Council of 1962 the Roman Catholic Church appeared to take a more liberal interpretation of natural law. Contrast the different attitudes of 1962 and 1995.

STRENGTHS OF NATURAL LAW

NATURAL RIGHTS - Enshrined in the American Constitution: "these truths we hold to be self-evident, life, liberty and the pursuit of happiness". So Natural Law gives a universal guide for judging whether an action is right or wrong as enshrined in key modern documents like the UN declaration of Human Rights (1948) or the European Convention of Human Rights (now passed into UK law as the Human Rights Act).

RATIONALITY - Natural Law is an autonomous, rational theory and it is wrong to say that you have to believe in God to make sense of it. Aquinas speaks of "the pattern of life lived according to reason". You could be a Darwinian atheist and believe in natural law derived by empirical observation, with the primary precept of survival (Aquinas' preservation of life). Dawkins go so far as to argue for a natural genetic tendency to be altruistic: a lust to be nice.

> *"The theory of Natural Law suggests ... morality is autonomous. It has its own questions, its own methods of answering them, and its own standards of truth ... religious considerations are not the point."*
> *Rachels (2006:5)*

FLEXIBILITY - In construction of secondary precepts. The secondary precepts are not absolute, but may change as our understanding of human nature develops.

WEAKNESSES OF NATURAL LAW

CONFUSES IS AND OUGHT - The combination of descriptive and normative elements. Aquinas seems to describe natural rational nature as something we observe most human beings following, and then says "we all ought to be like this". David Hume argues that you can't derive a value (preservation of life is good) from an observable fact (reasonable people all want to preserve life) without supplying the missing premise. Natural Law commits what we call the naturalistic fallacy.

REASON IS CULTURAL - Natural Law assumes that human nature and reasoning are identical. They're not. Different people in different countries and cultures think in different ways.

HUMAN NATURE ISN'T FIXED - Aquinas' view of human nature, that there is one, fixed nature cannot account for varieties of human tendencies (eg heterosexual and homosexual).

THERE IS NO PURPOSE - The randomness of the world depicted by modern science challenges the teleological idea of people moving towards a goal. Richard Dawkins argues "there is no purpose".

QUOTES

"Natural law is the sharing in the eternal law by intelligent creatures." Thomas Aquinas

"Every marital act must of necessity retain its intrinsic relationship to the procreation of human life ... this is a result of laws written into the actual nature of man and woman." Humanae Vitae, 1967

"Far from being a 'given', the idea of 'nature' is shaped by the prior assumptions of the observer. One does not 'observe' nature; one constructs it." Alister McGrath, 2001

"According to the religious view, what is behind the universe is more like a mind than anything else we know ... it is conscious, and has purposes, and prefers one thing to another. There is a something which is directing the universe, and which appears to me as a law urging me to do right." CS Lewis, Mere Christianity, pp. 16, 19, 33

"Every art and every investigation, every action and pursuit, is thought to aim at some good: and for this reason the good has rightly been declared as that to which all things aim." Aristotle

"It is because the ultimate end is implicit in every human action that Thomas can hold that natural law is valid for all men at all times." Ralph McInery, Ethica Thomistica, p. 47

"Granted that the world is ruled by divine providence ... that the whole community of the universe is governed by divine reason ... the very idea of the government of things in God the Ruler of the Universe has the nature of law. And since the divine reason's idea of things is not subject to time but is eternal ... therefore this kind of law must be called eternal ... because it is ordained by God to the government of things foreknown by him." Thomas Aquinas, Summa Theologica

"Precisely because of this 'truth' the natural law involves universality. Inasmuch as it is inscribed in the rational nature of the person, it makes itself felt to all beings endowed with reason and living in history. In order to perfect himself in his specific order, the person must do good and avoid evil, be concerned for the transmission and preservation of life, refine and develop the riches of the material world, cultivate social life, seek truth, practise good and contemplate beauty." (VS 51) Veritatis Splendor, 1995

SELF-TEST 1: KEY TERMS

- **NATURAL LAW**
- **DIVINE LAW**
- **HUMAN LAW**
- **TELEOLOGICAL WORLDVIEW**
- **DEONTOLOGICAL THEORY**
- **SYNDERESIS RULE**
- **PRIMARY PRECEPTS**
- **SECONDARY PRECEPTS**
- **PHRONESIS**
- **APPARENT GODS**
- **REAL GODS**
- **INTRINSIC GOD**

SELF-TEST 2: ANALYSIS

1. What is "natural" about Natural Law?

2. "Natural Law is a deontological theory based on a teleological worldview." Discuss.

3. Explain why synderesis (knowledge of good and evil) is an a priori self-evident concept.

4. How are primary precepts derived?

5. How are secondary precepts derived?

6. Using natural law theory, how does the Catholic Church argue against contraception?

7. What is the difference between a real and an apparent good?

8. What is the importance of phronesis (practical wisdom) in avoiding apparent goods?

9. Construct an argument for contraception using Natural Law theory.

10. Why might Natural Law theory be said to be not as absolute as sometimes suggested?

FURTHER READING

- **BUCKLE S** - in Singer ed., A Companion to Ethics, Blackwell (1995) Ch 13
- **JACKSON P** - in Dialogue 12 (April 1999) Natural Law
- **JONES ET AL** - (2002) pp. 100-104
- **MCINERY R** - Ethica Thomistica, Catholic UP (1997)
- **POJMAN L** - (2002) pp. 45-59
- **RACHELS J** - (2006) pp. 50-55
- **SUGGATE A** - Dialogue 5 (Nov 1995) Is There a Natural Law?
- **VARDY & GROSCH** - Puzzle of Ethics (1999) Ch 4

Deontology revisited

Deontology considers theories of duty and obligation which create rules. The deontological theories of Kant and Natural Law are often considered as non-consequentialist, absolute theories, but when we analyse these theories we find this to be over-simplified.

HOW ABSOLUTE IS DEONTOLOGICAL ETHICS?

Kantian ethics at least as presented by many summaries would appear to be an absolute theory of ethics in two senses. There is one absolute, non-negotiable method of deriving the good, known as the categorical imperative, and this is applied universally in all like relevant situations. There are no exceptions to its application. In this second sense whatever the circumstances might be the principle must be applied, such as"do not steal".

However, as we argued earlier, there is a debate among academics as to whether Kantian **CATEGORICALS** can admit of exceptions. For example, can we universalise a rule which says "always tell the truth, except when someone's life is at risk"? (The case of the crazy axe murderer discussed on pages 48-50.) Both Rachels and Schneewind suggest that such qualified universals are possible, although it seems to me Kant himself would reject such a possibility on the grounds that such categoricals become hypotheticals "tell a lie if you need to save a friend".

Natural Law theory has always maintained, at least in Aquinas' form, that secondary precepts are "proximate conclusions" or rules of thumb rather than hard and fast absolutes. Aquinas himself concedes that they may be changed by "addition" or "subtraction". For example, the idea of prohibiting abortion because it violates the primary precept of preservation of life might itself be modified if it could be established that the child born will suffer horrible pain. This would be an example of a "subtraction" or a dilution of the idea of the sanctity of human life.

Also the Roman Catholic ban on contraception could be modified in the face of evidence that AIDS in Africa is rising fast due to the no contraception policy.

This tells us something important about Natural Law deontology, namely that there is one **TELEOLOGICAL** principle that determines the nature of goodness. This principle is called **EUDAIMONIA**, which means a goal of personal and social flourishing. So any additions and subtractions that may occur in the application of natural law known as the **SECONDARY PRECEPTS** would need justifying according to the final end or telos of eudaimonia.

But what of the primary precepts themselves? We considered earlier how Veritatis Splendor, the papal document published in 1995 changed the primary precept of worship of God to "contemplation of beauty". This is rather a significant subtraction - admiring a beautiful Picasso is clearly not quite the same thing as prostrating oneself in front of a holy God.

And as far as additions go, the precept of showing concern for the environment was also added by the same document. This represents a shift from the view that humankind has "dominion over the earth" (Genesis), in favour of a gentler view. However, it falls some way short of arguing that the environment has intrinsic goodness, as Gaia theorists or deep ecologists might argue.

Finally, WD Ross is one of many theorists (JS Mill is another) who have argued for a non-absolute deontology. Beware of an ambiguity here, however. There is still one absolute idea of **INTRINSIC** goodness in Ross and Mill's view - that of happiness or pleasure. What is non-absolute, however is the application of Ross' prima facie rules, which only apply at first sight and not when all circumstances are taken into account, at least if there is a conflict of duties. Then, in cases of conflict, we will know by intuition, argues Ross, which duty takes precedence.

IS DEONTOLOGY OPPOSED TO CONSEQUENTIALISM?

Kantian deontology is often presented as opposed to consequentialism of the utilitarians. This too is an error. Mill himself argued that Kant was a utilitarian in disguise.

In truth, there is a consequentialist element to Kantian ethics that occurs in two ways. Firstly, when I universalise my behaviour I am thinking of the likely consequences for everyone and society generally if everyone acted in the same way. I make an imaginative consequentialist leap, especially when imagining a contradiction in will which asks the question: would I want to live in a world where everyone behaved like this?

Secondly, Kantian ethics has as its final goal the **SUMMUM BONUM** or greatest good. This is a situation existing in the afterlife where the fruits of everyone's good will are fully realised in world where virtue truly does have its own reward in happiness and harmony of heaven itself.

Now, this cannot be the motive for our action - the hope of achieving immortality - but is rather the byproduct of my dutiful obedience to the moral law derived by applying the categorical imperative.

It is nonetheless a consequence of so acting, even if not a motive, and does suggest that there is more consequentialism in Kantian ethics than is often conceded.

IS DEONTOLOGY REASONABLE?

Kantian deontology us based on the idea of a universal reason which all free human beings share. The moral law is universal because human reason is universal - it operates in the same way across time and culture.

But the Kantian idea faces two problems:

Reason is culturally specific, not neutral. The way postmodern man reasons is different from Enlightenment man. For example, Enlightenment man believes all truth is absolute, whereas postmodern man sees truth as relative.

The process of universalising actions is not a neutral process. I universalise from a particular standpoint according to my reading of the likely consequences. In this book I have argued that Kant does have a form of consequentialist thinking central to his argument - you cannot universalise without thinking of consequences.

So when Kant argues that we would all universalise the same sort of rational categorical maxims he is arguably wrong. There is nothing inconsistent in universalising the maxim "persecute those who are subhuman, such as Jewish people". This universalisation emanates from a sick Nazi ideology, and that is the point - it is perfectly rational from that particular standpoint.

As Alasdair MacIntyre concludes:

> *"... what Kant presented as the universal and necessary principles of the human mind turned out in fact to be principles specific to particular times, places and stages of human enquiry." (2006:266)*

What of Natural Law reason? Natural Law is built on an assumption of teleological purpose. Humans have a rational purpose built in to their very nature.

This purpose is grasped intuitively by an innate process called synderesis - we are born with a knowledge of the first principles or primary precepts of the natural law, and by nature we want to "do good and avoid evil".

The insights of Freud and the behaviourists (Skinner, Watson) would cast doubt on this version of the origins of human reason. They would argue that we are conditioned to behave in a certain way by our environment and upbringing. So just as Kant's appeal to pure reason fails because his own reason is a cultural construct, so Natural Law first principle of reason fails because it implies a shared, inherited a priori reason called **SYNDERESIS**.

Moreover, many Christians would argue that because of the Fall of Man we are incapable in our own natures of doing good. We are driven by selfishness and the desire for promotion of our own interests often at the expense of others. As Paul put it in Romans 7: "I do not do what I want, the evil I do not want, that's what I do."

If in fact I am driven by selfishness and this determines my goals, then the whole argument that the goals I pursue are naturally good falls apart.

Postscript

Peter Baron studied PPE at Oxford University and a Masters degree at Newcastle in Philosophy. He trained as an Economics teacher in 1982 and was ordained a priest in 1993. He returned to teaching full time in 2006 (Ethics and Philosophy). Peter has authored many books on Philosophy and Ethics and currently speaks at day conferences in schools around the country as diverse as Archbishop Tenison's, London and Dene Close, Cheltenham. His vision is to unite the best and most creative teachers from the state and private sector to inject new life into the classroom and create A-grade possibilities for all, irrespective of background and location.

Lightning Source UK Ltd.
Milton Keynes UK
UKOW04f0622271014

240674UK00002B/34/P